Owl

Remember Me Series

By

Caroline Norsk

Remember me I am an owl.

Remember me I am a bird.

Remember me I can be found all over the world.

Remember me I like to hunt alone.

Remember me I go, "Hooh-hooh-hooh!"

Remember me I can stare at you with really big eyes.

Remember me I can turn my head all the way around.

Remember me I can hear really well.

Remember me my hooked beak can rip.

Remember me I love to eat insects, animals, and birds that are smaller than me.

Remember me my beak is small but my mouth is big.

Remember me my wings can spread so wide.

Remember me I can also be so cute and small.

Remember me I hunt for food at night.

Remember me I can be gray, brown, and even snowy white.

Caroline Norsk

Remember me I can also be a friend.

18

Remember me I can lay 3 eggs.

Remember me I can help eliminate pests.

Remember me I can send letters from castle to castle from across the land.

Remember me in the morning, I yawn and go to sleep.

Thank you.

Good Luck.

Made in the USA
Middletown, DE
25 April 2018